In Celebration of:

_____

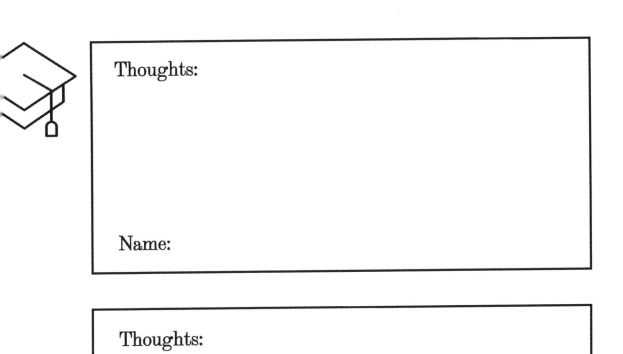

Thoughts:

Name:

Thoughts:

Name:

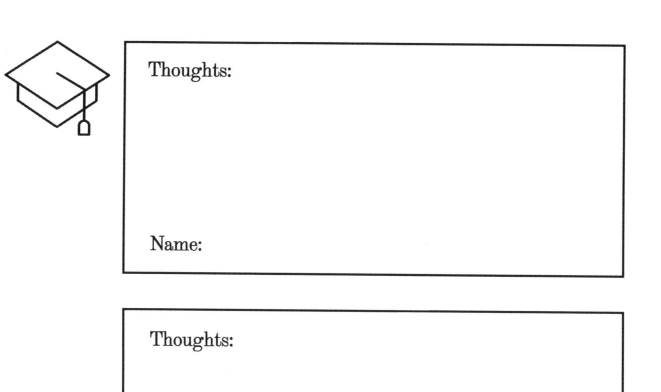

Thoughts:

Name:

Thoughts:

Name:

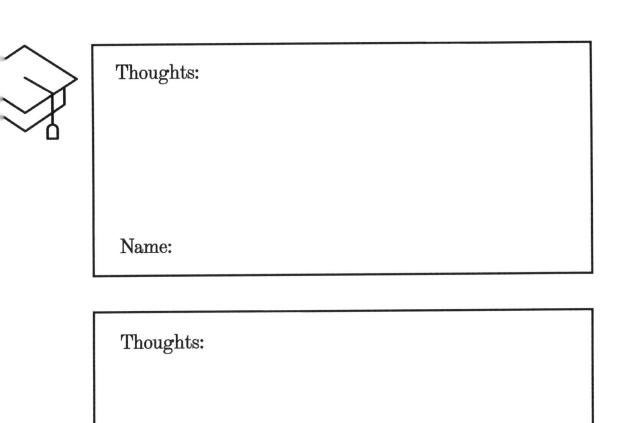

Thoughts:

Name:

Thoughts:

Name:

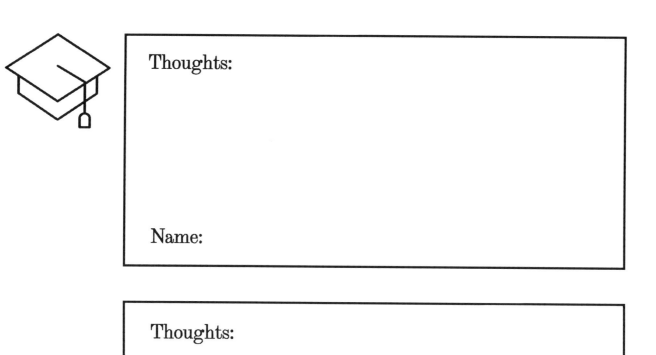

Thoughts:

Name:

Thoughts:

Name:

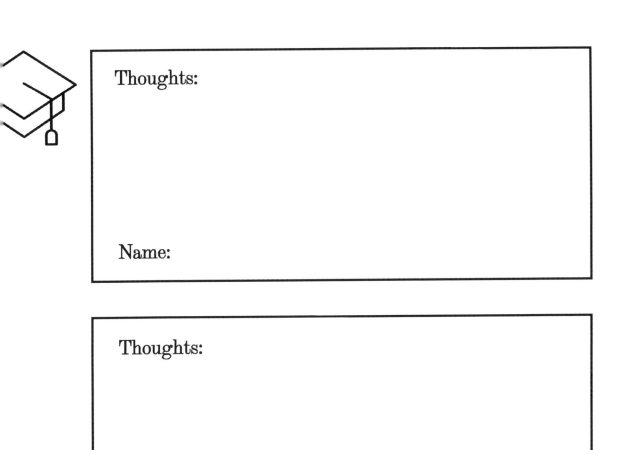

Thoughts:

Name:

Thoughts:

Name:

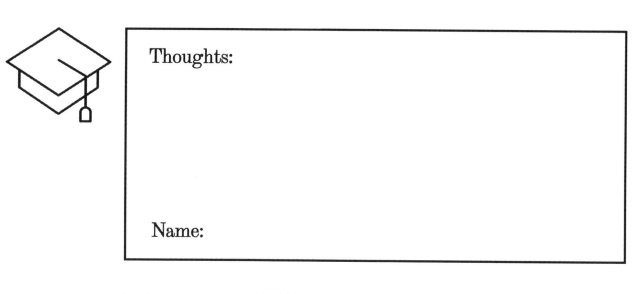

Thoughts:

Name:

Thoughts:

Name:

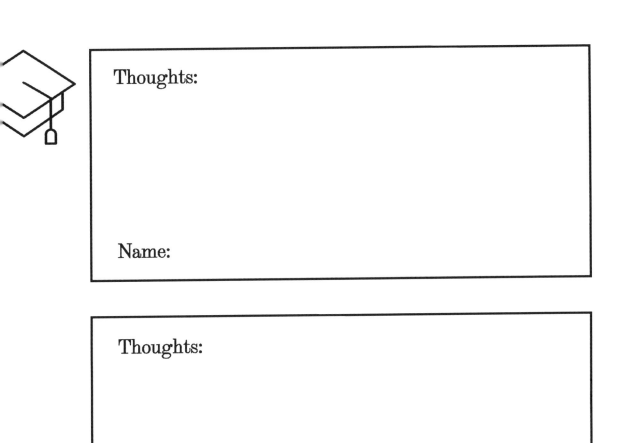

Thoughts:

Name:

Thoughts:

Name:

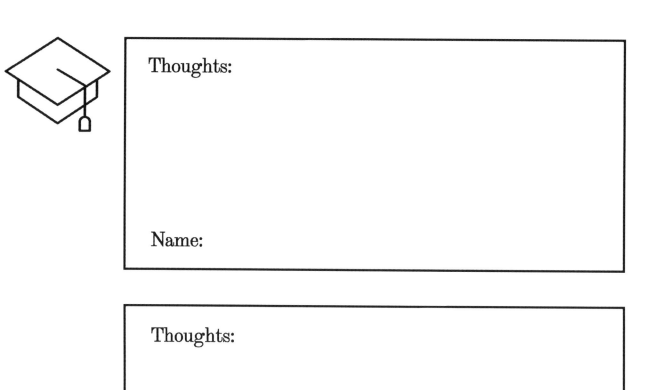

Thoughts:

Name:

Thoughts:

Name:

Thoughts:

Name:

Thoughts:

Name:

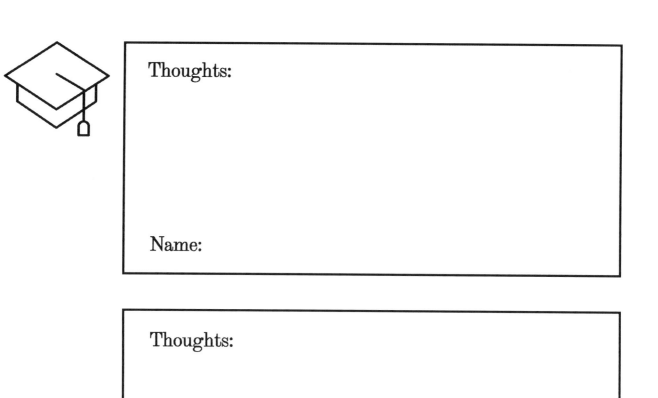

Thoughts:

Name:

Thoughts:

Name:

Thoughts:

Name:

Thoughts:

Name:

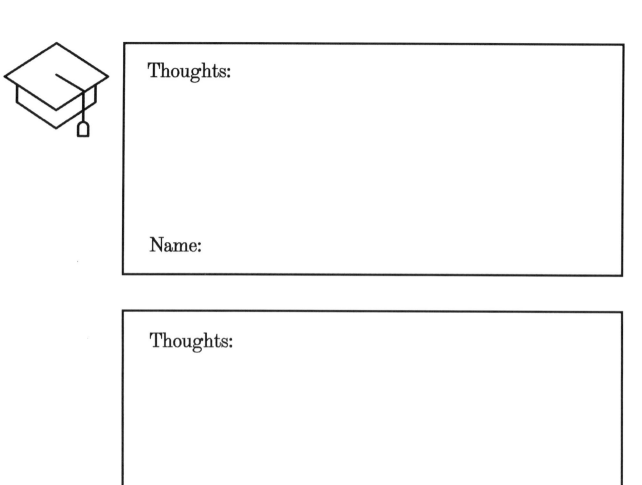

Thoughts:

Name:

Thoughts:

Name:

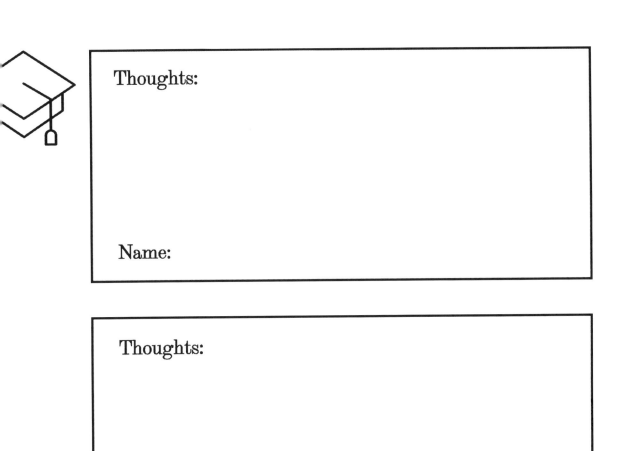

Thoughts:

Name:

Thoughts:

Name:

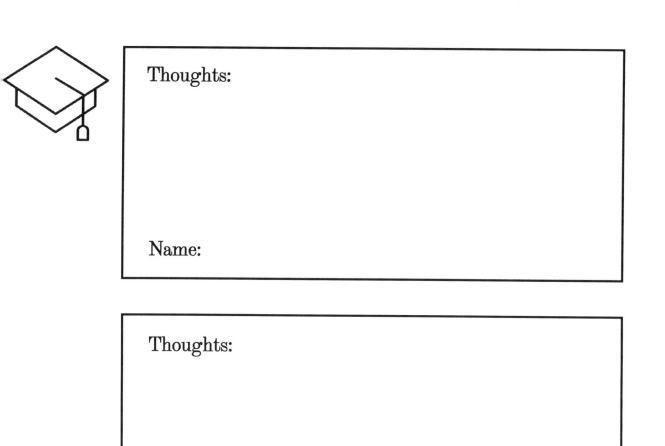

Thoughts:

Name:

Thoughts:

Name:

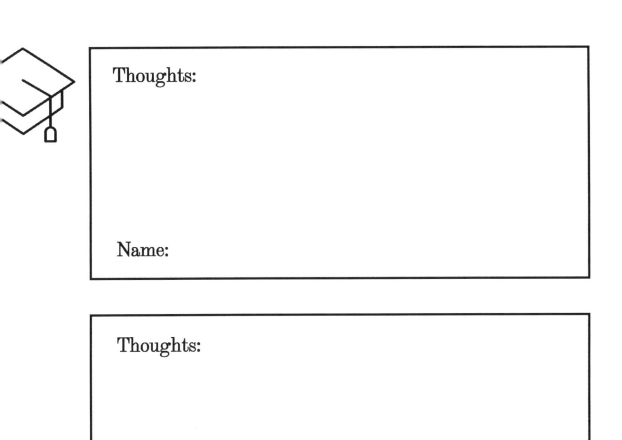

Thoughts:

Name:

Thoughts:

Name:

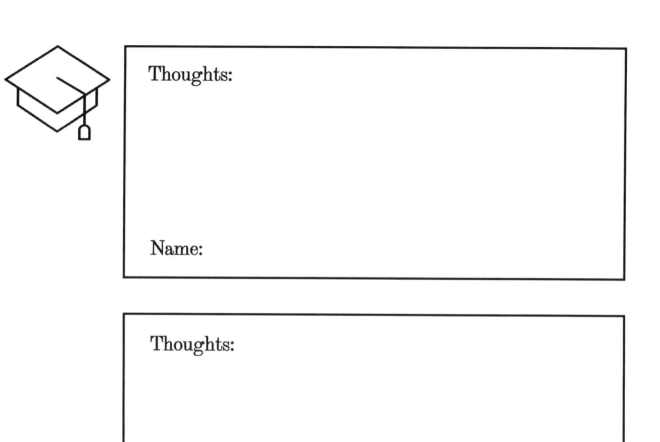

Thoughts:

Name:

Thoughts:

Name:

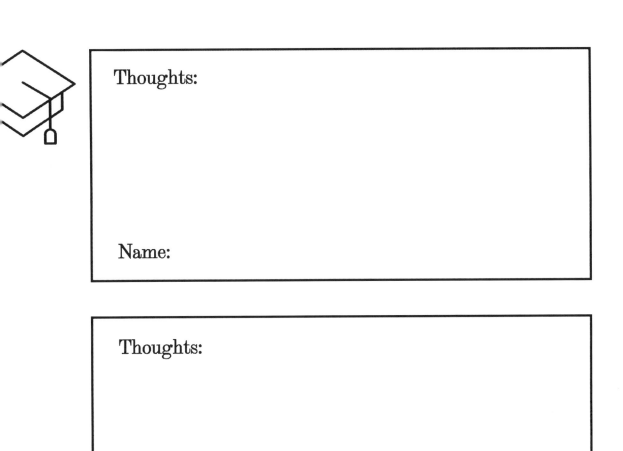

Thoughts:

Name:

Thoughts:

Name:

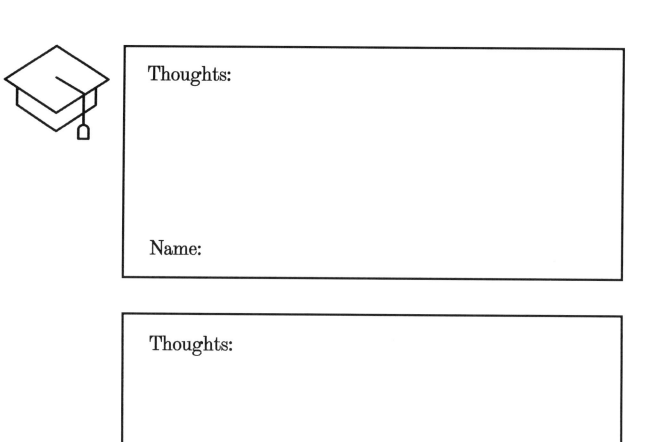

Thoughts:

Name:

Thoughts:

Name:

Thoughts:

Name:

Thoughts:

Name:

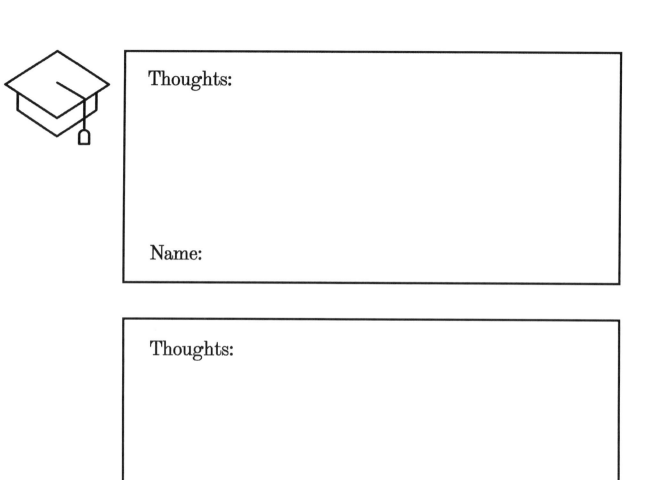

Thoughts:

Name:

Thoughts:

Name:

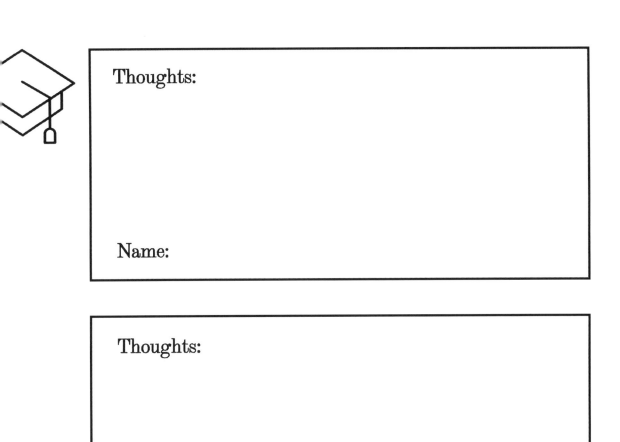

Thoughts:

Name:

Thoughts:

Name:

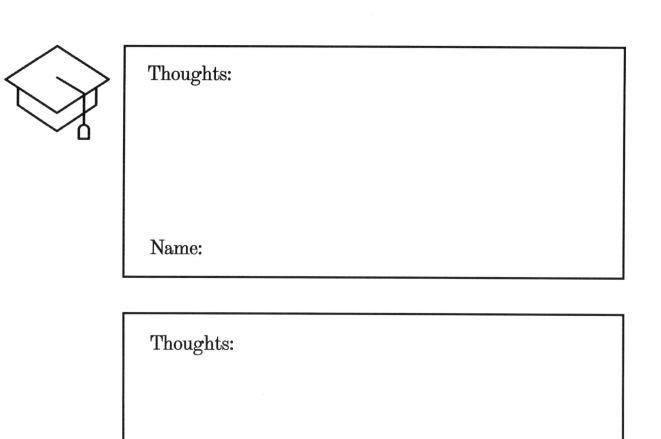

Thoughts:

Name:

Thoughts:

Name:

Thoughts:

Name:

Thoughts:

Name:

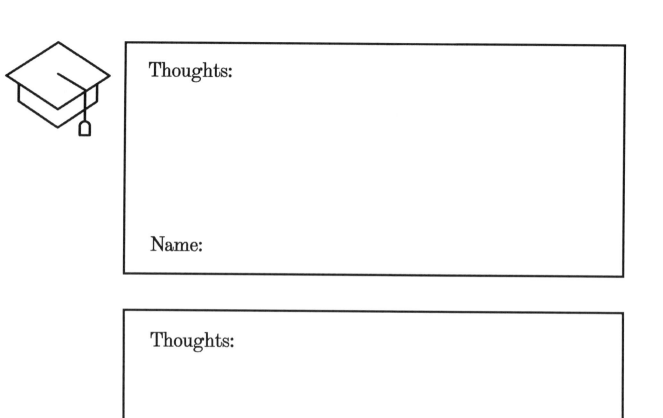

Thoughts:

Name:

Thoughts:

Name:

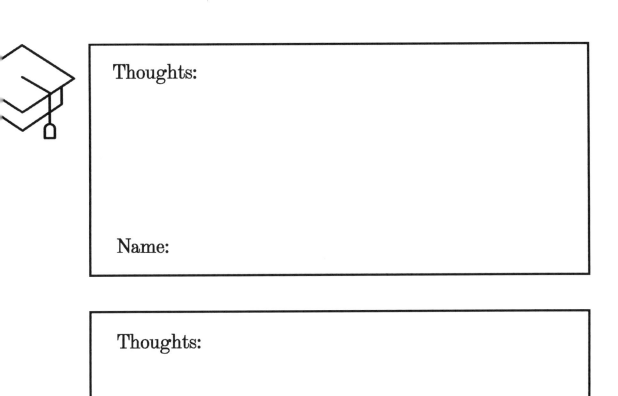

Thoughts:

Name:

Thoughts:

Name:

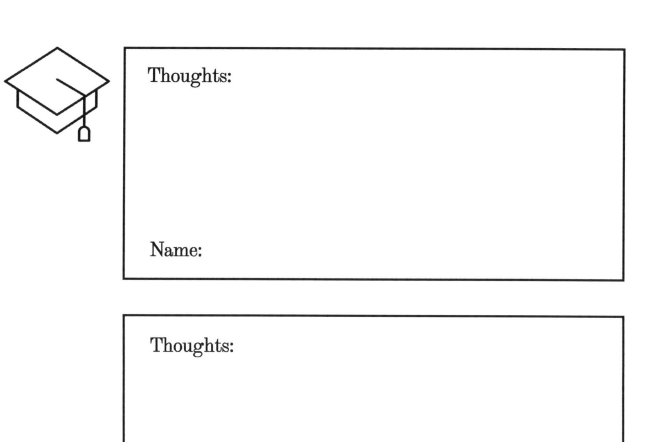

Thoughts:

Name:

Thoughts:

Name:

Thoughts:

Name:

Thoughts:

Name:

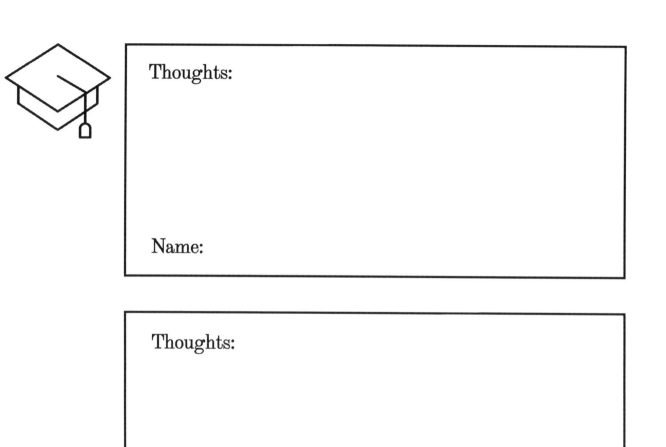

Thoughts:

Name:

Thoughts:

Name:

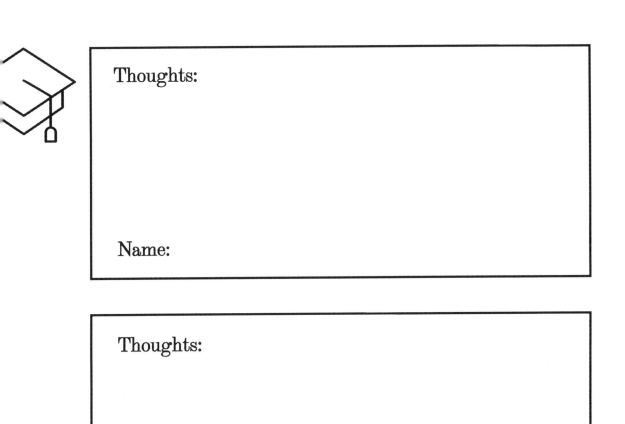

Thoughts:

Name:

Thoughts:

Name:

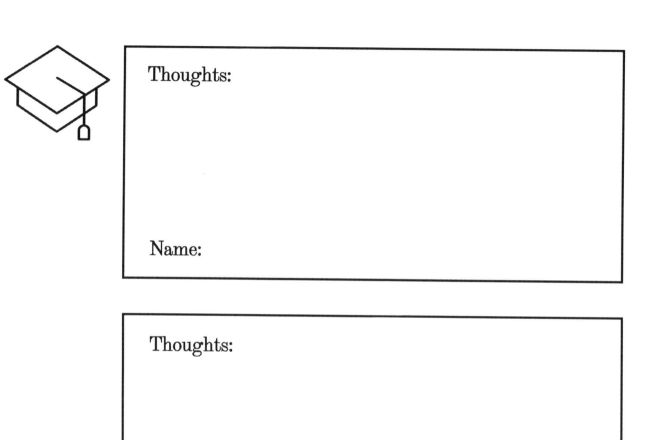

Thoughts:

Name:

Thoughts:

Name:

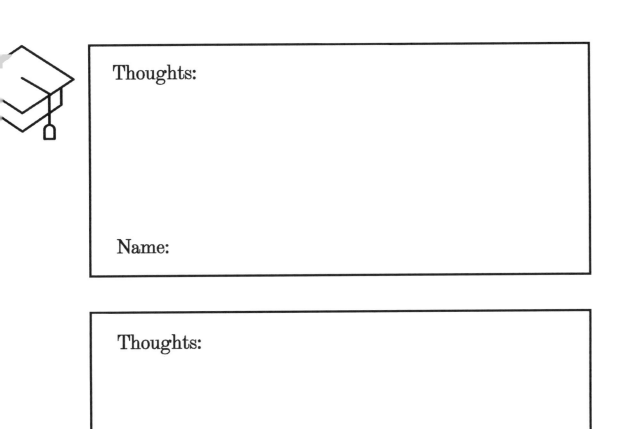

Thoughts:

Name:

Thoughts:

Name:

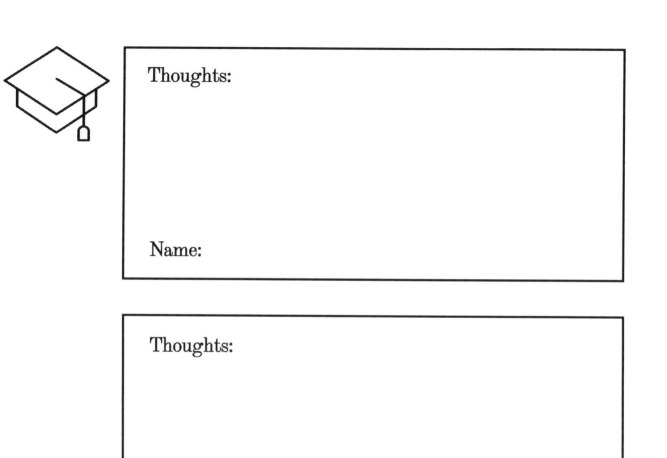

Thoughts:

Name:

Thoughts:

Name:

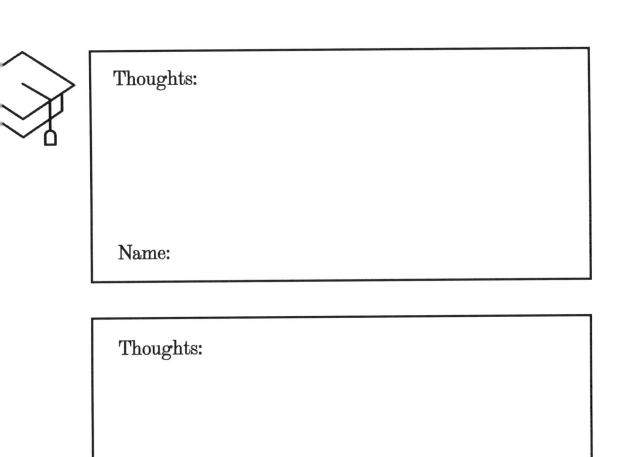

Thoughts:

Name:

Thoughts:

Name:

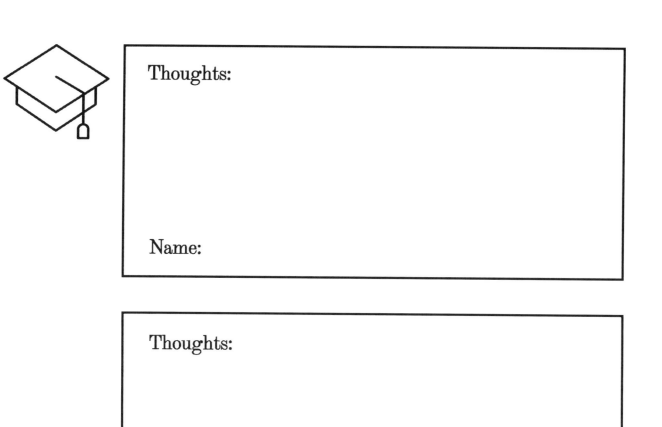

Thoughts:

Name:

Thoughts:

Name:

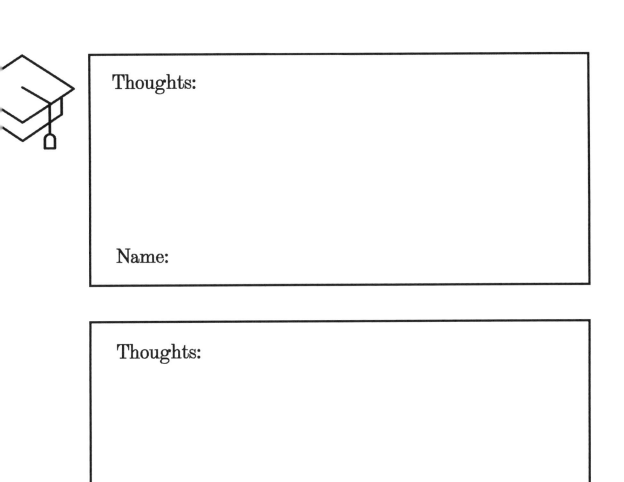

Thoughts:

Name:

Thoughts:

Name:

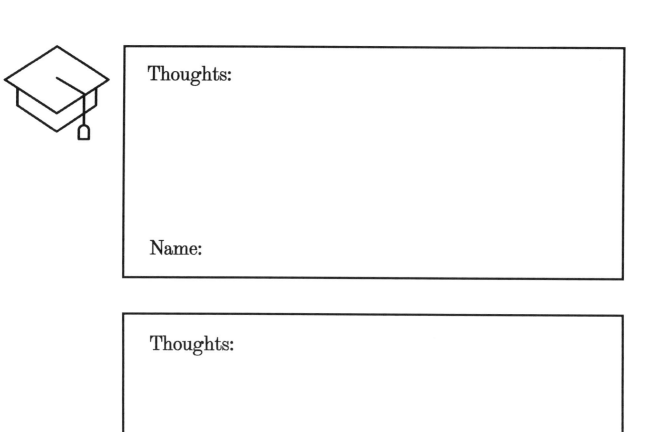

Thoughts:

Name:

Thoughts:

Name:

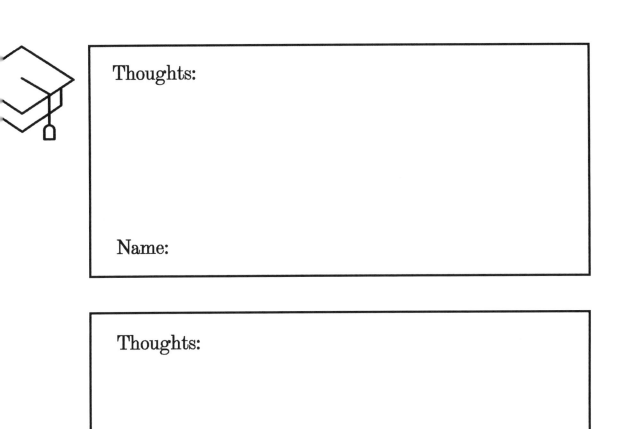

Thoughts:

Name:

Thoughts:

Name:

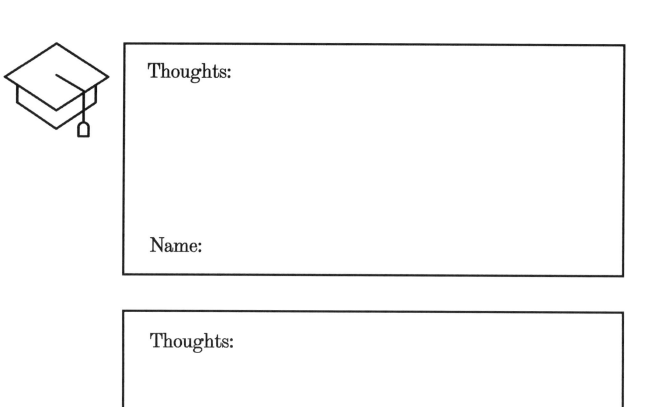

Thoughts:

Name:

Thoughts:

Name:

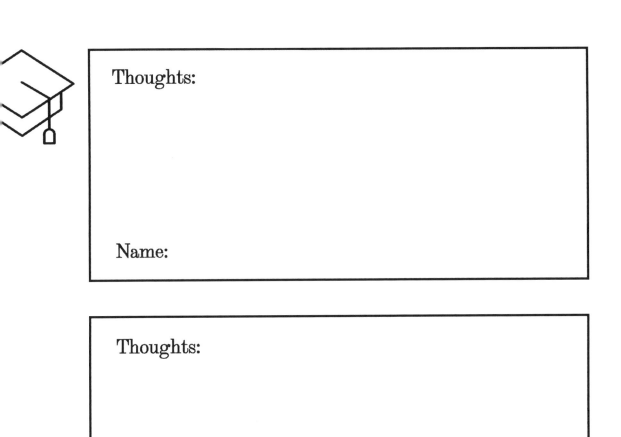

Thoughts:

Name:

Thoughts:

Name:

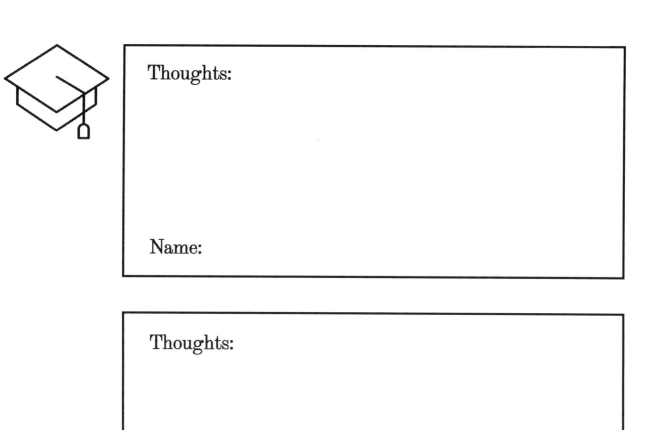

Thoughts:

Name:

Thoughts:

Name:

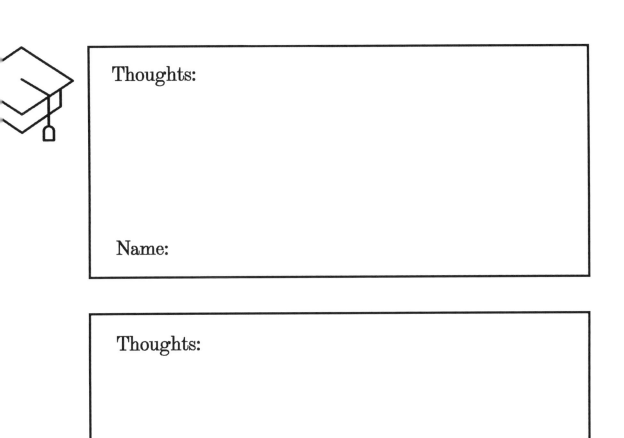

Thoughts:

Name:

Thoughts:

Name:

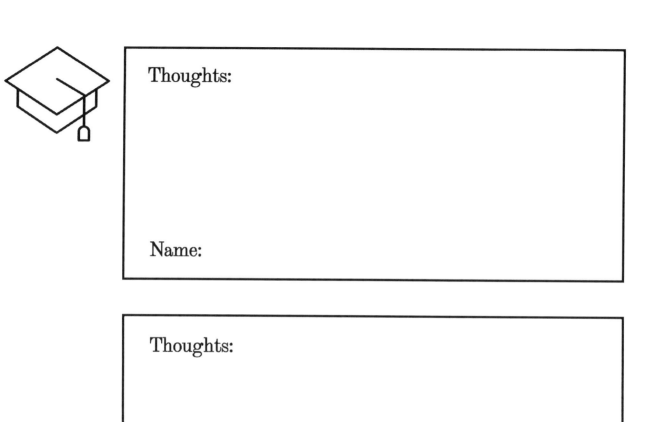

Thoughts:

Name:

Thoughts:

Name:

Thoughts:

Name:

Thoughts:

Name:

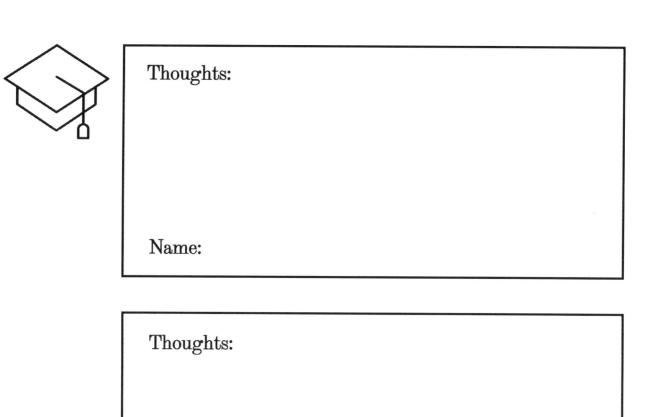

Thoughts:

Name:

Thoughts:

Name:

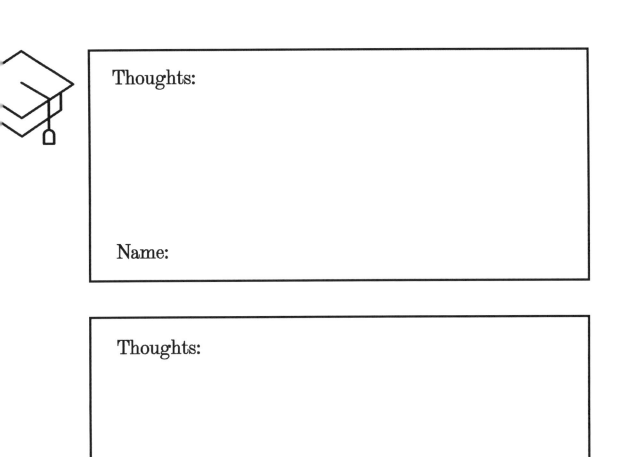

Thoughts:

Name:

Thoughts:

Name:

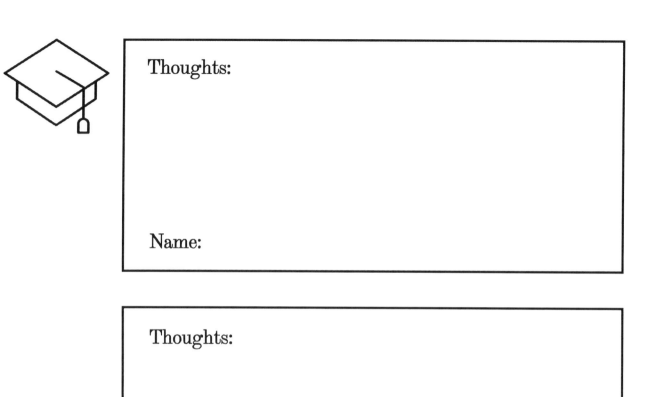

Thoughts:

Name:

Thoughts:

Name:

Thoughts:

Name:

Thoughts:

Name:

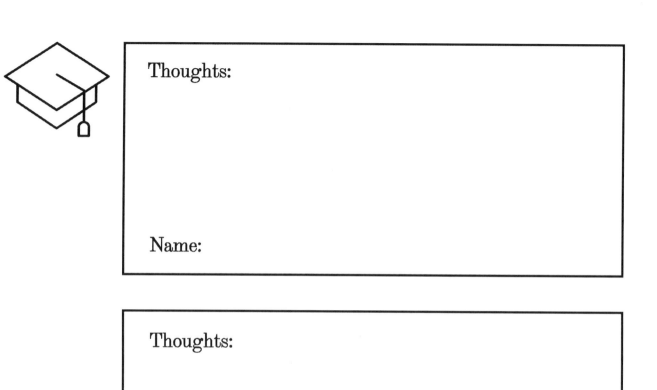

Thoughts:

Name:

Thoughts:

Name:

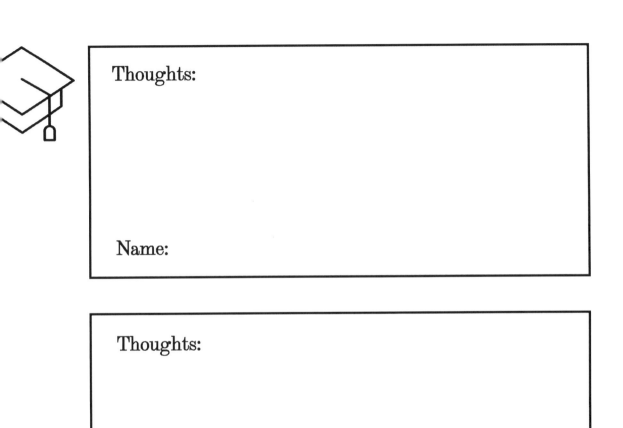

Thoughts:

Name:

Thoughts:

Name:

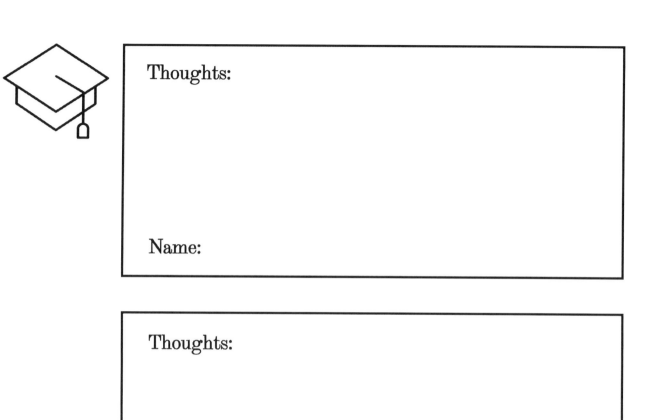

Thoughts:

Name:

Thoughts:

Name:

Thoughts:

Name:

Thoughts:

Name:

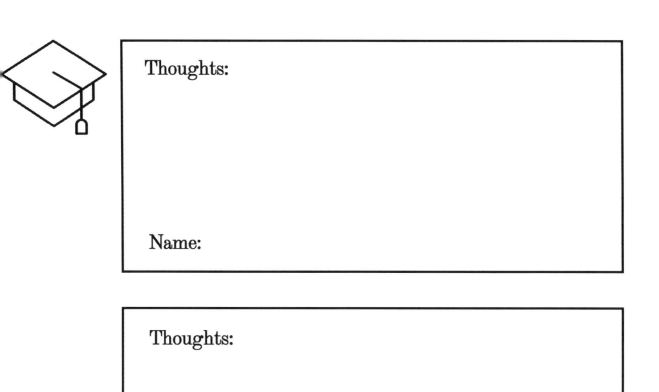

Thoughts:

Name:

Thoughts:

Name:

Thoughts:

Name:

Thoughts:

Name:

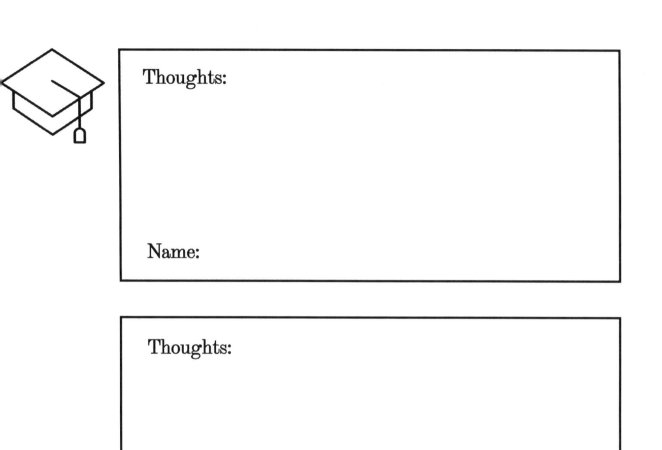

Thoughts:

Name:

Thoughts:

Name:

Thoughts:

Name:

Thoughts:

Name:

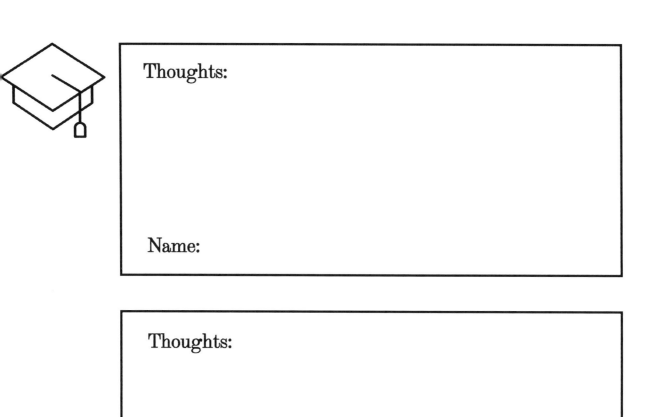

Thoughts:

Name:

Thoughts:

Name:

Thoughts:

Name:

Thoughts:

Name:

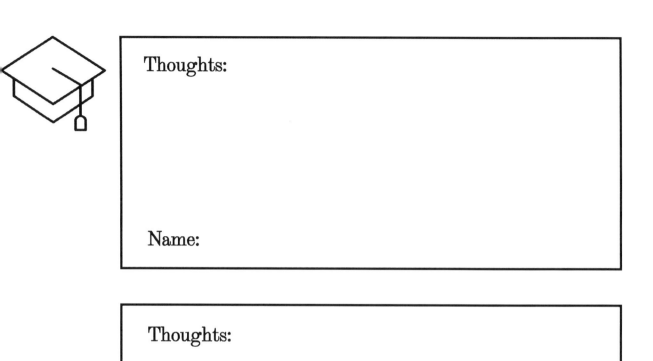

Thoughts:

Name:

Thoughts:

Name:

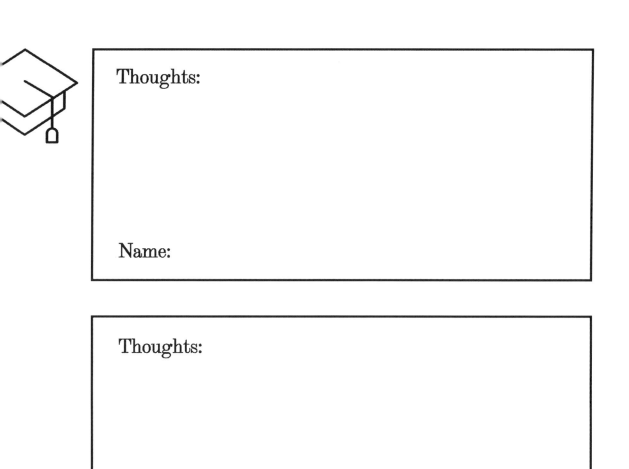

Thoughts:

Name:

Thoughts:

Name:

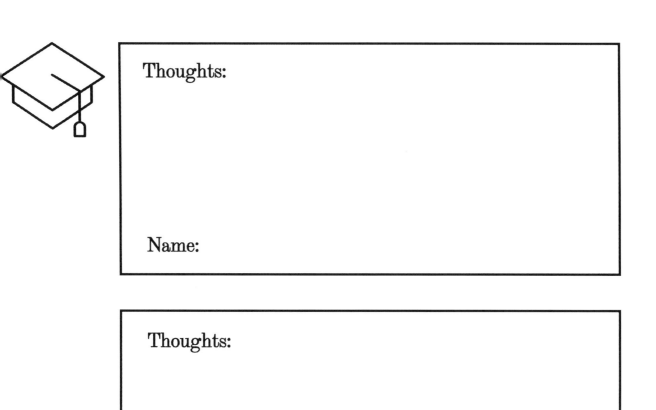

Thoughts:

Name:

Thoughts:

Name:

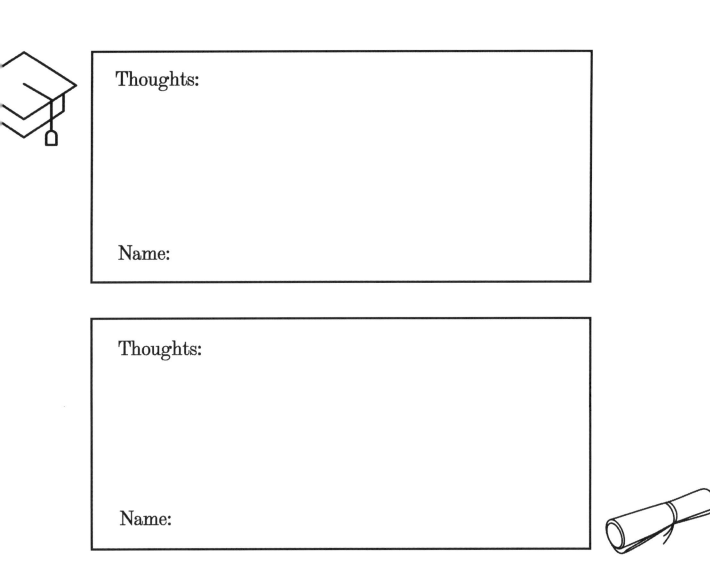

Thoughts:

Name:

Thoughts:

Name:

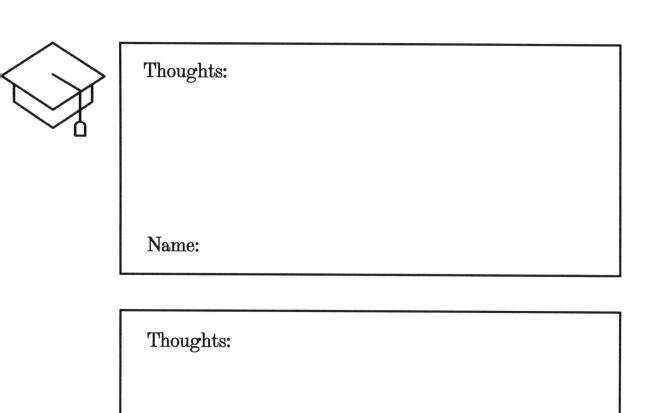

Thoughts:

Name:

Thoughts:

Name:

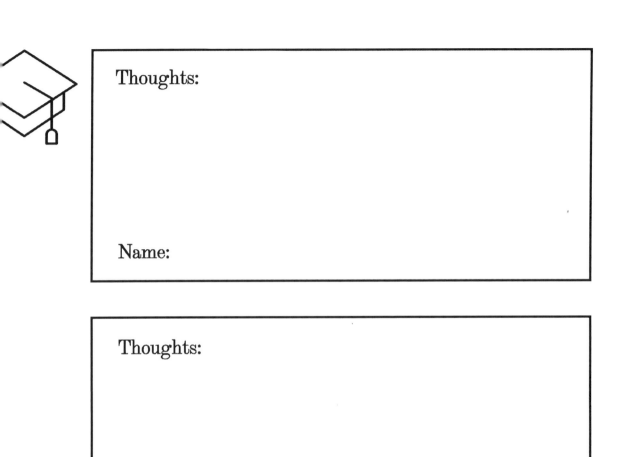

Thoughts:

Name:

Thoughts:

Name:

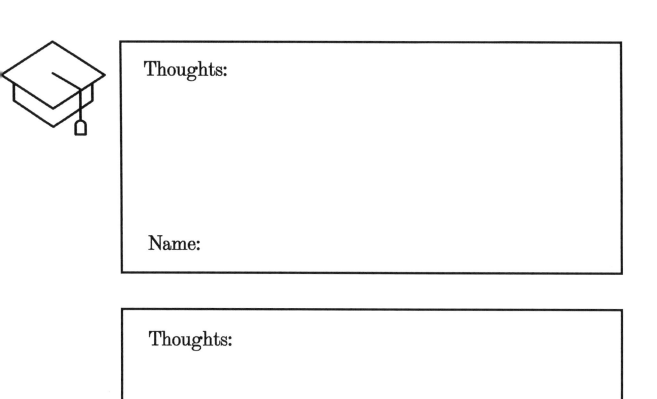

Thoughts:

Name:

Thoughts:

Name:

Thoughts:

Name:

Thoughts:

Name:

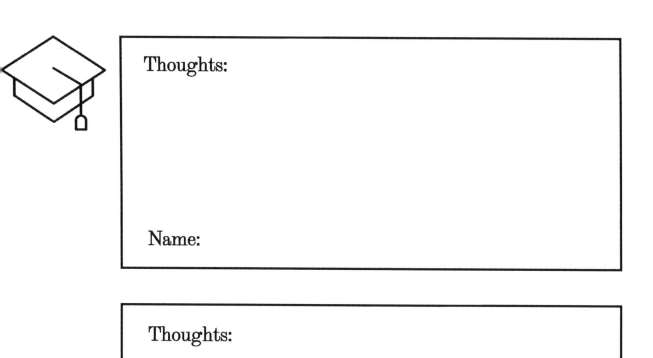

Thoughts:

Name:

Thoughts:

Name:

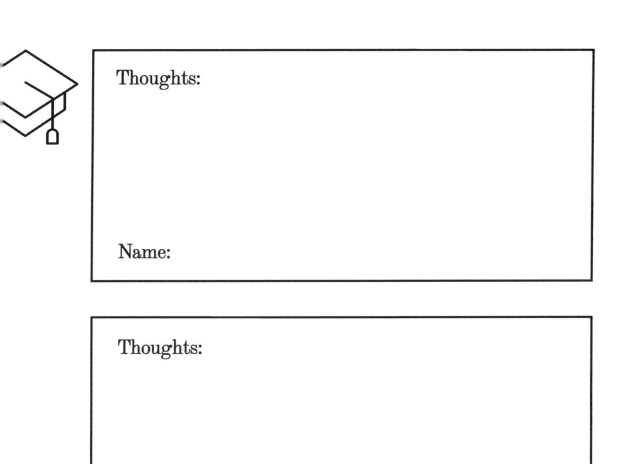

Thoughts:

Name:

Thoughts:

Name:

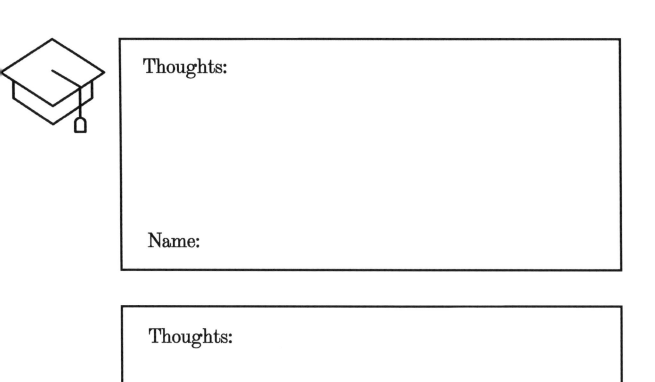

Thoughts:

Name:

Thoughts:

Name:

Thoughts:

Name:

Thoughts:

Name:

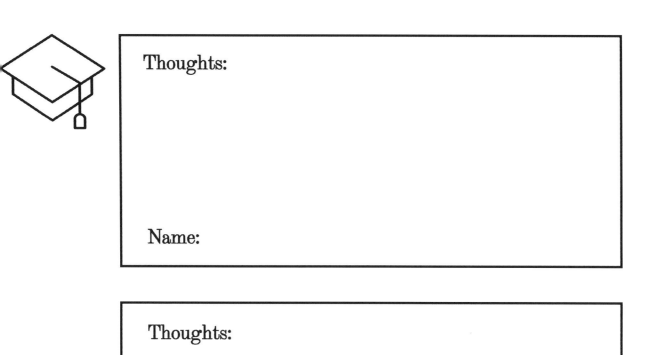

Thoughts:

Name:

Thoughts:

Name:

Thoughts:

Name:

Thoughts:

Name:

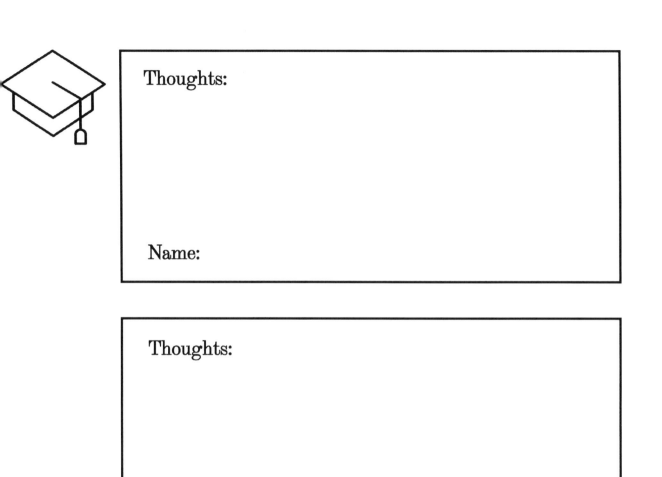

Thoughts:

Name:

Thoughts:

Name:

Thoughts:

Name:

Thoughts:

Name:

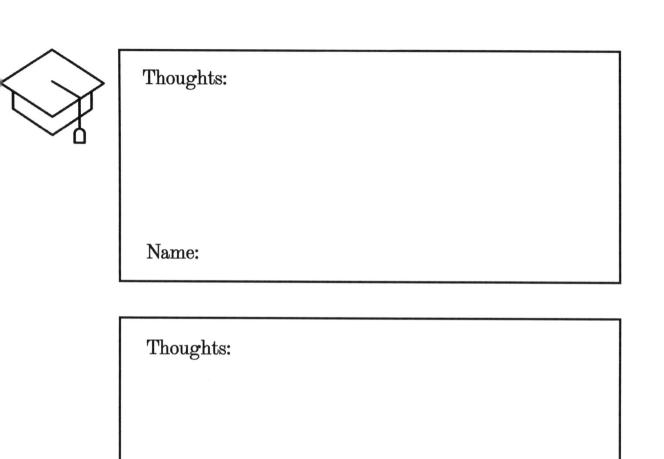

Thoughts:

Name:

Thoughts:

Name:

Thoughts:

Name:

Thoughts:

Name:

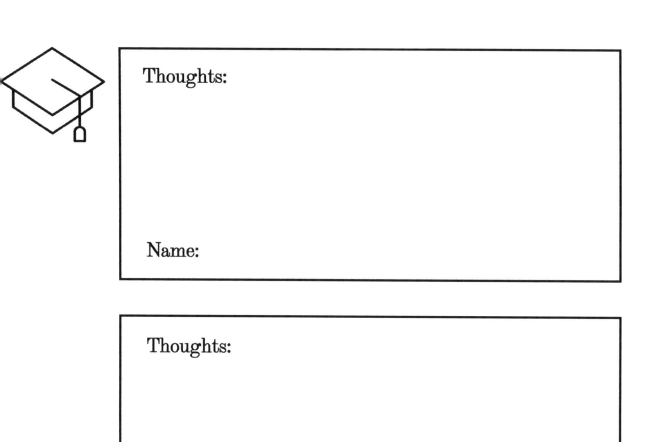

Thoughts:

Name:

Thoughts:

Name:

Thoughts:

Name:

Thoughts:

Name:

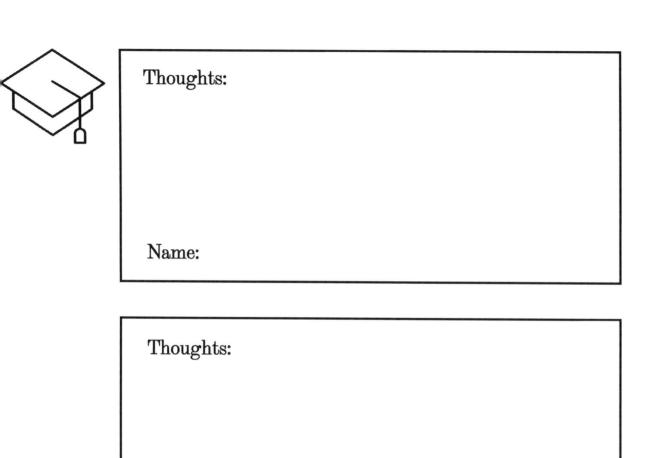

Thoughts:

Name:

Thoughts:

Name:

Thoughts:

Name:

Thoughts:

Name:

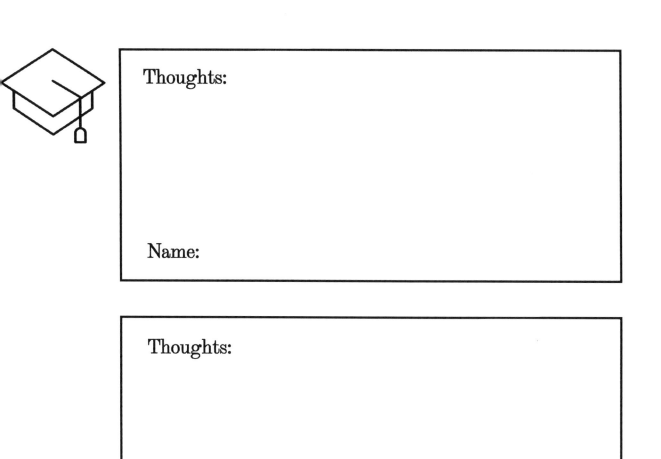

Thoughts:

Name:

Thoughts:

Name:

Thoughts:

Name:

Thoughts:

Name:

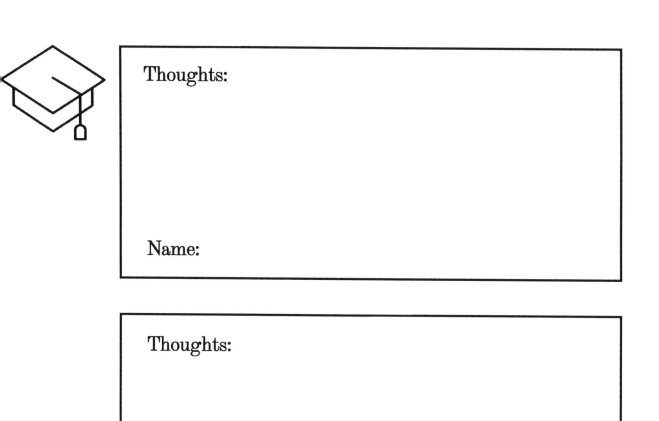

Thoughts:

Name:

Thoughts:

Name:

Thoughts:

Name:

Thoughts:

Name:

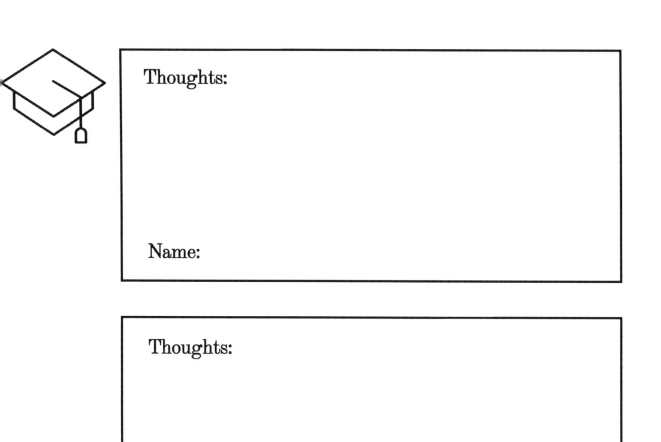

Thoughts:

Name:

Thoughts:

Name:

Thoughts:

Name:

Thoughts:

Name:

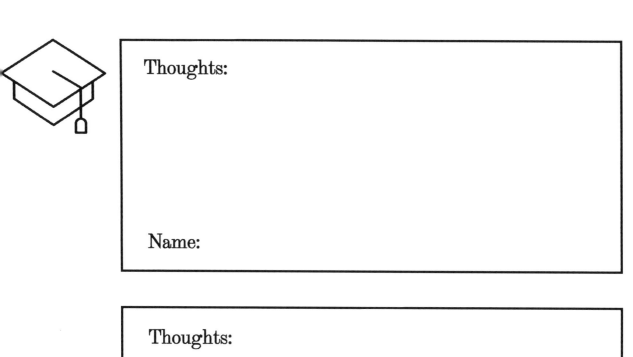

Thoughts:

Name:

Thoughts:

Name:

Thoughts:

Name:

Thoughts:

Name:

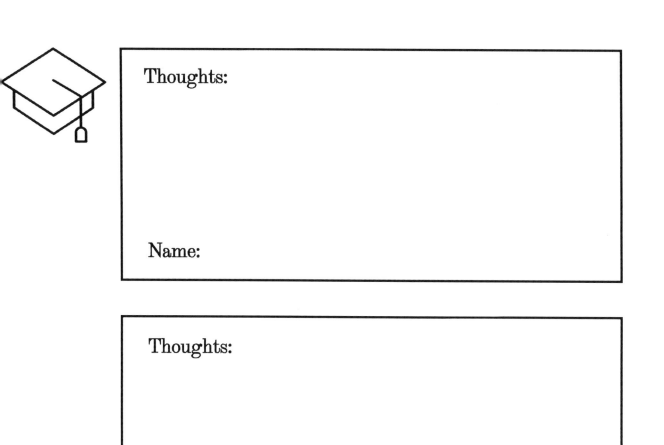

Thoughts:

Name:

Thoughts:

Name:

Thoughts:

Name:

Thoughts:

Name:

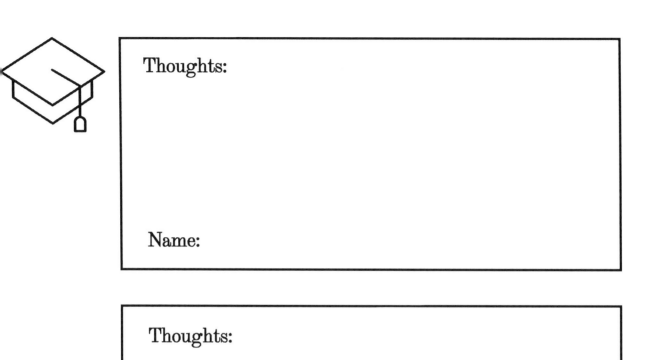

Thoughts:

Name:

Thoughts:

Name:

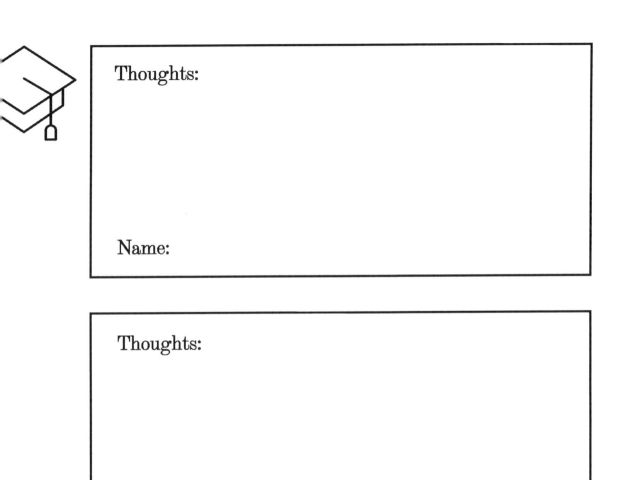

Thoughts:

Name:

Thoughts:

Name:

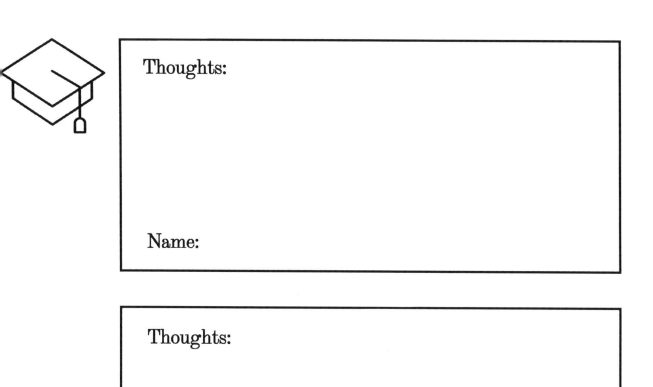

Thoughts:

Name:

Thoughts:

Name:

Thoughts:

Name:

Thoughts:

Name:

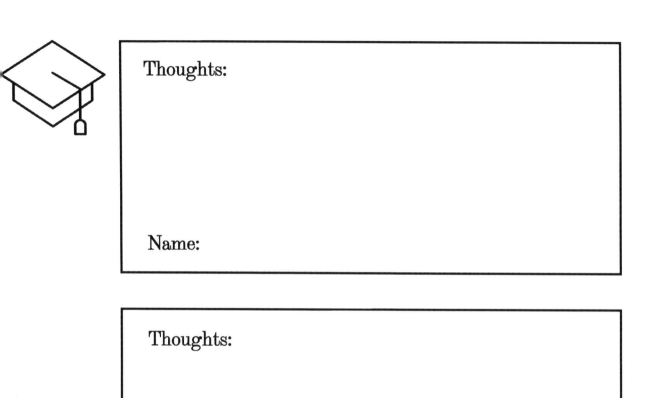

Thoughts:

Name:

Thoughts:

Name:

Thoughts:

Name:

Thoughts:

Name:

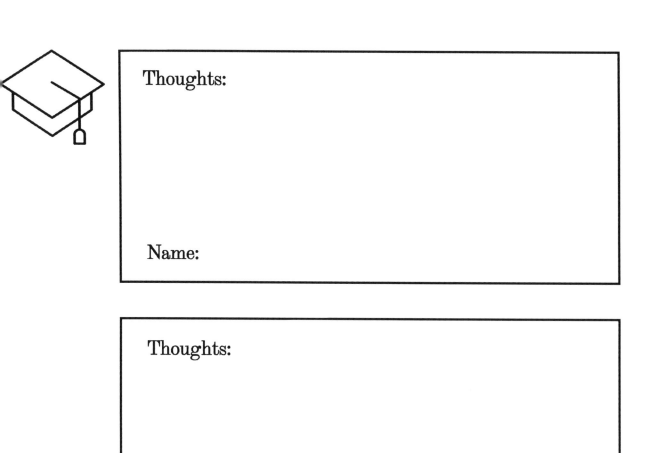

Thoughts:

Name:

Thoughts:

Name:

Thoughts:

Name:

Thoughts:

Name:

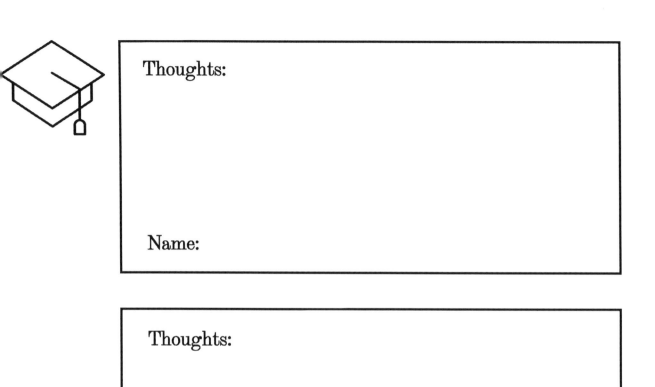

Thoughts:

Name:

Thoughts:

Name:

Thoughts:

Name:

Thoughts:

Name:

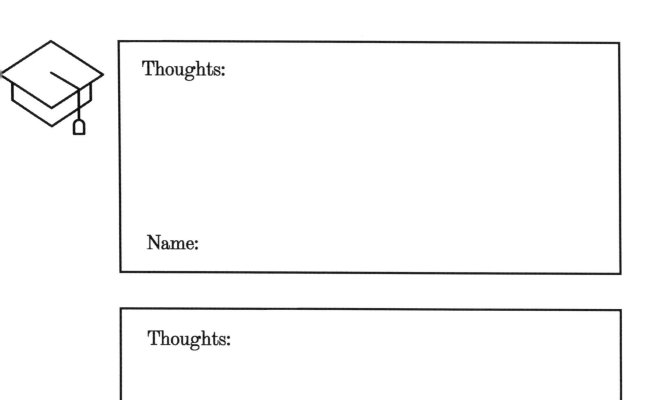

Thoughts:

Name:

Thoughts:

Name:

Made in the USA
Columbia, SC
23 October 2022

69886613R00057